Dressage for Beginners

Dressage for Beginners

R. L. V. ffrench Blake

A SEELEY SERVICE BOOK

Frederick Warne

Published by
Frederick Warne (Publishers) Ltd

First published 1973 (Seeley Service & Co. Ltd)
Reprinted with revisions 1976
Reprinted 1980

ISBN 0 7232 2624 5

Printed in Great Britain by
Hollen Street Press Ltd at Slough, Berkshire

1370·180

Contents

List of Illustrations

Preface

For some twenty years, I have been concerned in judging, teaching, watching, and riding dressage. In every novice competition there always seem to be a few who appear not to know what they are trying to do; it is to them that this book is addressed, as well as to those who have not yet started "doing dressage", but who for one reason or another, are going to get involved with the art.

This little book may help them to know what it is all about and on what lines they should start work.

"He who does not know the aim, cannot know the way".

* * *

Since the publication of the first edition, the F.E.I. Rules have been rewritten and certain practices in Britain have been revised in line with the F.E.I. Where the sense of the F.E.I. rules has not been changed, I have allowed the original wording to remain, but where there has been significant change, I have adopted the new wording.

Midgham Park Farm
Woolhampton

V ff B

Acknowledgements

I should like to thank Messrs Methuen and Co for permission to quote from, and to adapt some of the drawings from Wilhelm Müseler's "Riding Logic".

The following have read my MS in its early stages, and have provided invaluable criticism, comment, and encouragement—Molly Sivewright, Joan Gold, and the B.H.S. National Instructor, Bill Froude.

I am most grateful to Richard Scollins, who drew all the illustrations and diagrams, for his patient and skilful effort to turn my amateur scribbles into accurate and instructive pictures.

V ff B

Cover photograph by Neil ffrench Blake

Chapter 1

The requirements

There are two sides to dressage—the preparation of the horse, according to a set of well-established principles; and the presentation of the horse, from time to time, before judges, in competition.

This second element—the dressage "test"—is secondary, and incidental to the first. What matters is the work of rider and horse; the test will help to show progress, to establish standards, and to subject the rider's methods and their results, to informed and expert examination. Yet, without the tests, the rider will be working in a vacuum, without ambition, and without a target for his or her efforts.

There are many definitions of dressage, but since we are to work towards satisfying an official panel of judges, it will be as well to take the official definition, by the international equestrian authority, (the F.E.I.) which can be found in "Dressage Rules and Official Procedure for Dressage Competitions", published by the British Horse Society at 25p.

This definition gives the object of Dressage as

> "... harmonious development of the physique and ability of the horse. As a result it makes the horse calm, supple, and keen, thus achieving perfect understanding with its rider".

The definition continues by describing the qualities required:

a " — freedom and regularity of the paces
— harmony, lightness and ease of movements
— lightening of the fore-hand and engagement of the hind quarters.
— the horse remaining absolutely straight in any movement along a straight line, and bending accordingly when moving on curved lines".

b "The horse thus gives the impression of doing of his own accord what is required of him. Confident and attentive, he submits generously to the control of his rider".

c "His walk is regular, free and unconstrained. His trot is free, supple, regular, sustained and active. His canter is united, light, and cadenced. His quarters are never inactive or sluggish; they respond to the slightest indication of the rider, and thereby give life and spirit to all the rest of his body".

d "By virtue of a lively impulsion and the suppleness of his joints, free from the paralysing effects of resistance, the horse obeys willingly and without hesitation, and responds to the various aids calmly and with precision".

e "In all his work, even at the halt, the horse must be on the bit. A horse is 'on the bit' when the hocks are correctly placed, the neck is more or less raised, according to the extension or collection of the pace, the head remains steadily in position, the contact with the mouth is light, and no resistance is offered to the rider".

f "The position of the horse when 'on the bit' depends on the conformation as well as the degree of training of the horse".

The definition then goes on to give in detail the requirements for the different paces, and for all the movements, from the basic paces, up to the most advanced stages.

The general definition given above is a most carefully phrased statement—every word is of significance, and the students of dressage cannot read it too often, nor should they neglect the detailed definitions of the particular movements which follow in the Rule Book.

What is your image of dressage? An arena of white boards and letters, with an interminable series of the Pony Club or Novices plodding round all day?—the compulsory ordeal which Combined Training competitors must undergo before they can do their jumping and cross-country?—the classical but sometimes archaic teamwork of the Spanish Riding School or the Cadre Noir?

In fact, all these are part of the same art; one stage of training leads to another, and riders may go as far on the road to perfection as they want, and as ability of rider and horse permits.

The tests issued by the British Horse Society fall into the following standards: Preliminary, Novice, Elementary, Medium, Advanced.*

Broadly speaking, the additional requirements are as follows:

*Early in 1974 all B.H.S. tests were revised to conform with F.E.I., using "collected", "working", "medium" and "extended" paces (see Glossary. The rein-back was deleted from Novice Tests and the walk pirouettes from Elementary Tests. The term "ordinary" walk, trot or canter is no longer used. The easier British tests are less advanced than their Continental equivalents.

Preliminary: basic paces, free walk on long rein, circles of 20 metres diameter at trot and canter. Progressive transitions i.e. from trot to halt through a few paces of walk.

Novice: circles of 15 metres diameter, serpentines at trot, lengthened strides at trot. Walk half-circles 3-5 metres diameter. Transitions less progressive.

Elementary: circles of 10 metres at trot, medium trot, extended walk, circles of 15 metres at canter, canter serpentine with some counter-canter, medium canter. Transitions direct from walk to canter, trot to halt. Simple change at canter through walk.

Advanced elementary: collected trot and canter, shoulder-in at trot, canter circles of 10 metres.

Medium: collected walk, trot and canter, trot circles of 8 metres, counter-canter round end of arena, half-pass at trot, transitions from extended to collected pace at trot and canter. Rein back, half pirouettes at walk.

Advanced medium: trot circles of 7 metres, canter circles of 8 metres, half-pass at canter, single flying changes.

Advanced: trot zig-zags at half pass (counter-change of hand), canter serpentine with flying changes, half-pirouettes at canter, four-time flying changes. Transitions from canter to halt.

For competitions above this standard the British Horse Society uses the following international tests

Prix St Georges: trot circles of 6 metres (voltes), counter-canter circles of 10 metres, canter zig-zags at half-pass with flying changes. Flying changes every four strides.

Intermediate: canter pirouettes, four, three and two-time flying changes.

Grand Prix de Dressage: one-time flying changes, *piaffe* and *passage*.

It will be seen that Preliminary, Novice and Elementary stages contain the basic requirements of schooling for every form of riding horse, whatever the purpose for which it is to be used; Medium standard is for the rider who needs an intensely active and supple horse, e.g. Three-Day Event horses, polo ponies, show jumpers. Advanced Dressage is a specialised art, and the horse which reaches this stage will probably not be used for anything else.

The scope of this book is concerned only with helping the beginner to enter on the first stages.

Let us pause then, to extract from the complicated language of the definition, the bare essentials with which to begin our work on the horse. The rider may have a young, untouched, or 'green' horse, or more likely a 'spoilt' horse, wrongly schooled by other, less knowledgeable riders; almost certainly a 'puller', neck upside-down, one-sided, with one or more bad habits well engrained. It makes little difference; it is better to start from the beginning in either case; the horse is a creature of habit, and the instilling of good habits can overlay and eradicate bad ones. In any case, dressage involves not only controlling the behaviour of the horse but also developing the correct muscles, and allowing muscles incorrectly used to waste away. An example of this is the neck; a pulling horse normally adopts this attitude

Fig. 1. An unschooled horse

—head too high and 'above the bit'; and a bulge of muscle, in the front of the lower part of the neck, is used to resist all efforts of the rider to lower his head, or to reduce speed.

Make the experiment of standing at the horse's head and lowering his head into the correct position by offering him a handful of food. With the other hand feel the muscle at the front of the neck, which will be quite soft and relaxed.

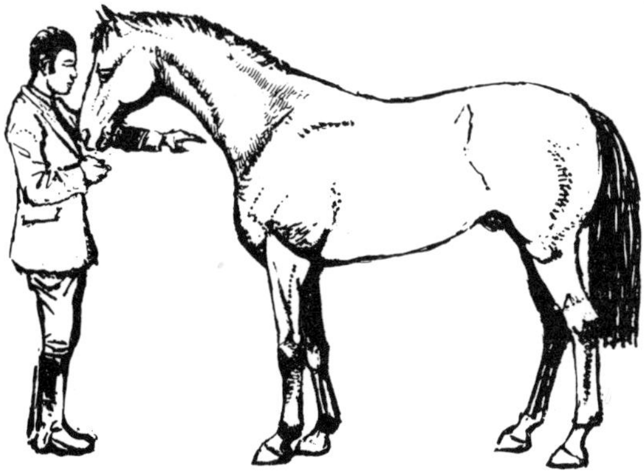

Fig. 2. Relaxing the lower muscles of the neck

Now, if the horse can be persuaded (not forced) to carry his head in this position, the bulge of muscle, no longer permanently in tension, will gradually atrophy and fade away to its proper proportions, and the horse will be not only better-looking—but also will have a much better 'mouth'.

To return to the search for the essential steps: first are

1. Relaxation.
2. Correct gait, with regular rhythm, at each pace.
3. Free forward movement.
4. Straightness.

later will come

5. Suppleness—correct bends.
6. Attitude—including head carriage.
7. Improvement of the basic paces.

later still

8. Cadence.
9. Collection.

We shall consider each of these steps in turn in the following chapters.

Chapter 2

Starting work

Before starting work, the rider must have the right equipment. Novice dressage is performed in a plain snaffle, with either cavesson or dropped nose-band; no martingale is allowed; a whip may be carried,* except in Combined Training competitions. A list of permissible types of snaffle is given in the Rules. A long dressage whip is essential, since it can be applied without taking the hands off the reins.

It is impossible to sit correctly in the wrong saddle; most old-fashioned hunting saddles put the rider too far back; if possible, get a modern type of saddle in which the rider sits comfortably in the lowest part of the seat. The waist of the saddle should also be narrow, allowing the rider to have a 'deep' seat, and thus a close feeling of the horse.

We shall not yet need an arena, though a confined space is useful, and if there is no access to a covered school or enclosed *manège*, the rider can mark out a rectangle, preferably rather larger than the standard small arena of 40 metres (44 yards) x 20 metres (22 yards). Pegs or oil drums can define an area of flat ground about 60 x 30 yards.

We now come to the question of the rider's seat. This cannot be learnt by reading, though an indication of what is required will be found in many text-books. One of the clearest and most explicit descriptions can be found in Wilhelm Müseler's *Riding Logic* (Methuen).

The only real answer is to go to a good Instructor, and get your seat put right; and from time to time, go back, and check that you

* The use of whips is still under review in Britain.

have not acquired bad habits. Even the most experienced of riders subject themselves to this constant criticism. Without a correct seat, much work and time will be wasted. To quote Captain Stefan Skupinski, a well-known Polish Instructor working in this country: "if rider will be right, horse will be right". The converse is true, if the rider sits wrongly, the horse will develop faults.

Various types of seat are shown below:

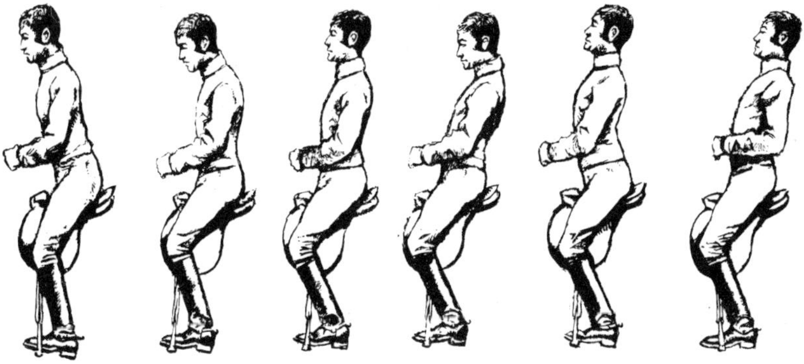

(a) (b) (c) (d) (e) (f)

Fig. 3. (*a*) *Leaning forward on the fork.* (*b*) *Slack back—head poked forward.* (*c*) *Correct—upright, riders' centre of gravity balanced over that of the horse.* (*d*) *Back braced—correct for driving forward, or in downward transitions.* (*e*) *Stiff back—bottom sticking out.* (*f*) *Leaning back, reins too long.* To which we may add some local variations: *Fig. 4.* (*g*) "*Hunting seat*"*—lower leg thrust forward.* (*h*) "*Cavalry crouch*"*—rounded back.* (*j*) *Weight on the back of the saddle.* (*k*) *Above the saddle, standing on stirrups*

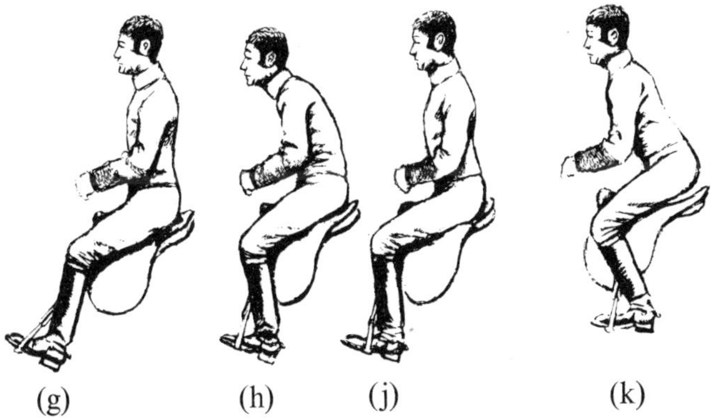

(g) (h) (j) (k)

In working the horse for the initial stage, we shall aim first of all at relaxation; the horse must be prepared to go calmly at any pace, allowing the rider to give a loose rein and retake it without altering pace, to walk, trot, or canter round the school or arena without rushing or getting excited. It may be necessary to achieve this by sheer boredom, hour after hour of persuading the excitable* horse that it is not going anywhere else, that it is not to be upset by other horses passing by, or by strange sights and sounds. *Until this state of relaxation is achieved, it is no use attempting anything else.* With relaxation will come the second most important factor, an even regular rhythm; that is to say, the feet at any pace coming to the ground with the regularity of a metronome, in four-time at the walk (one-two-three-four); two-time (one-two, one-two) at the trot; and three-time at the canter. The rider's own rhythm must be as steady as that of his mount, or he may unbalance the horse, as yet unstable.

We can now work for free forward movement.

Once we have relaxation and rhythm, we can then concentrate upon the correct speed at any gait, encouraging the sluggish horse to more energy, persuading the over-eager to drop into a slower 'tempo', without sacrificing the freedom of movement. The sluggard must be conditioned to response to the rider's leg—not by incessant banging and squeezing with the leg, but by a sharp tap with the whip the instant that there is a lack of reaction to the aid.

During this early work, the horse must be kept straight at all times, particularly during the transitions from one pace to another, and when halting. The rider must not halt or reduce speed by merely pulling on the reins, but by sitting 'with' the horse, driving a little on to the bit, and carrying out the transition almost by thinking about it, rather than by any violent application of the aids. In 'downward' transitions, i.e. canter to trot, trot to walk, the rider must brace the back to avoid tipping forward at the change of pace.

Colonel Podhajsky, former head of the Spanish Riding School, when working in Britain, was asked to give lessons to some riders with novice horses. "Take them away" he would say, "go out into the country and work the horse on straight lines, responding properly to the leg, I can teach nothing until that has been done."

One sees many horses in dressage competitions, pulling against the rider, cantering far too fast, fighting into the halts and downward transitions. One longs to ring the bell and say "take it away, and

* Many horses are excited by over-feeding.

come back when you can trot and canter quietly round the arena on a loose rein".

When the horse is moving forward freely, rhythmically, and relaxed, we can consider the next stage, which is to teach the horse to move in curves, accepting a bend to right and left, and for this we can start using the arena. Naturally we shall not confine all our work to the enclosure, but will alternate with rides on the road or in the country, or horse and rider will soon become stale; in addition, riding in the open will take us over rough ground, up and down hills, and into places where the horse will learn to balance himself under the weight of the rider.

Chapter 3

Using the arena

For novice tests, we shall always use the small arena*, which consists of two squares of 20 metres forming a rectangle 40 x 20 metres.

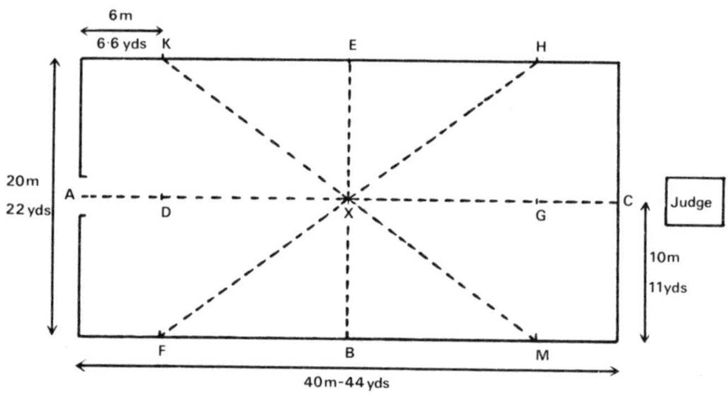

Fig. 5. The small arena

The centre-line is marked AC, the half-markers on the long sides are E and B, and there are four markers at 6 metres from the end of the long sides, KHMF, marking the diagonals across the school and also defining the straight length of the long side. Normally, the rider should not start to turn the corner until after passing these markers. The centre is marked by X, and the points on the centre line at 6 metres from the ends are D and G. (D is seldom marked). The centre line is marked with sawdust or whitewash, or by being lightly mown.

The arena may be marked by continuous boards, intermittent boards, or a white line with pegs at the corners. Entry and exit is by an opening at A—*never* over the boards.

* The large arena is 60 x 20 metres, and is used for the F.E.I. Three-Day Event test, Advanced and most International tests.

To construct a simple arena, see Appendix II.

All tests start with an entry at A, a halt and salute at X, followed by a move-off to C, where the rider 'tracks' right or left round the arena, 'on the right or left rein'.

Riding through the corners

When we start to ride in the arena, the first problem that arises is how to go round the corners. The trained horse should be bent throughout its whole length, to fit the curve on which it is travelling.

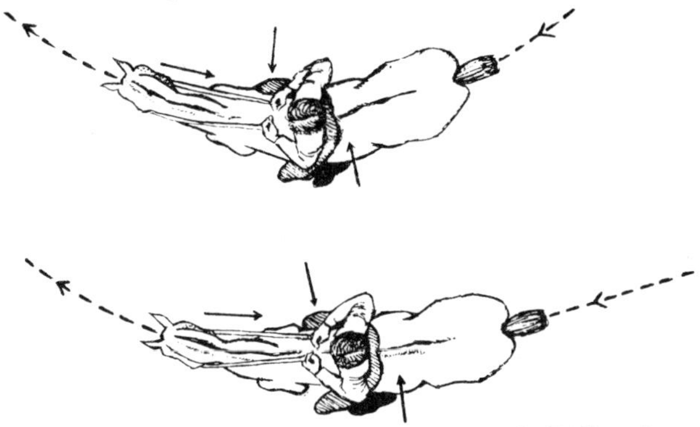

Fig. 6. Riding in a curve

The inside rein supported by a yielding outside rein bends the neck, the rider's outside leg, drawn a little back, bends the quarters round the inside leg, or if you like, the inside leg pushes the centre outwards. The effect should be to ensure that the track of the hind legs follows exactly in that of the forelegs. The outside rein supports, and controls the speed.

Obviously, a stiff horse cannot bend as much as a supple one, and therefore cannot describe so small a circle. All corners should be ridden as a quarter circle, and the rider should only go as deep into the corner at any pace, as can be managed without losing the rhythm.

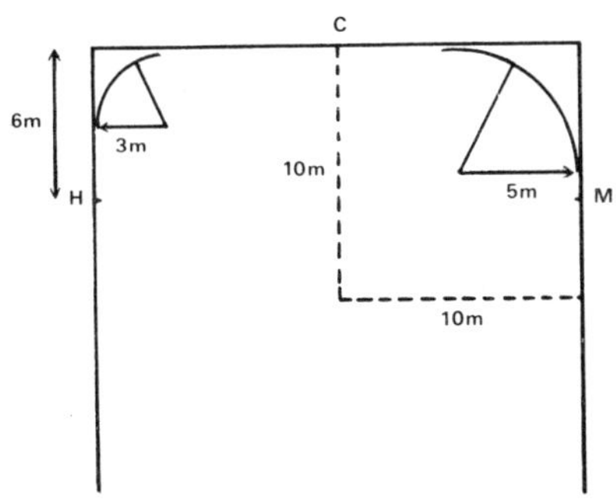

Fig. 7. Riding through the corners

A fully trained horse, at advanced standard, can canter collected through a corner on a radius of 3 metres, i.e. the quarter of a circle of 6 metres in diameter—as above, left. Above right is a corner of 5 metre radius, i.e. part of a 10 metre circle.

A good novice horse should be able to walk deep into the corner at 3 metre radius, trot at 5 metre radius, and canter at 6 metre radius, thus:—

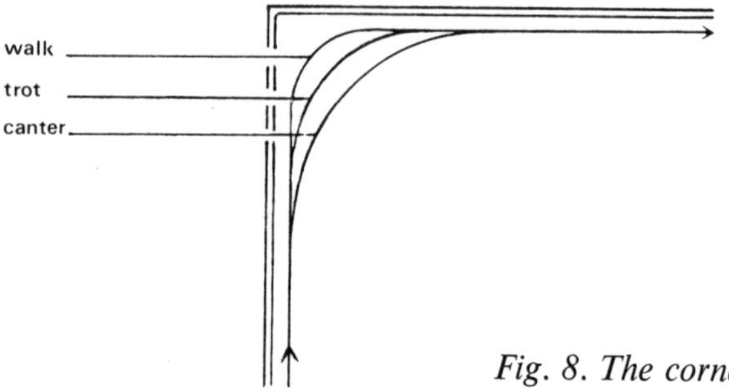

Fig. 8. The corner at different paces

But at first this will probably not be possible, since the green horse and the spoilt horse will probably not accept the bend at all, but when the rider goes round the corner, the horse will 'fall in', that is, drop its shoulder inwards, and look outwards; when the rider tries to establish the bend the horse will leave the track inwards. Generally, it will be stiffer on one side than on the other.

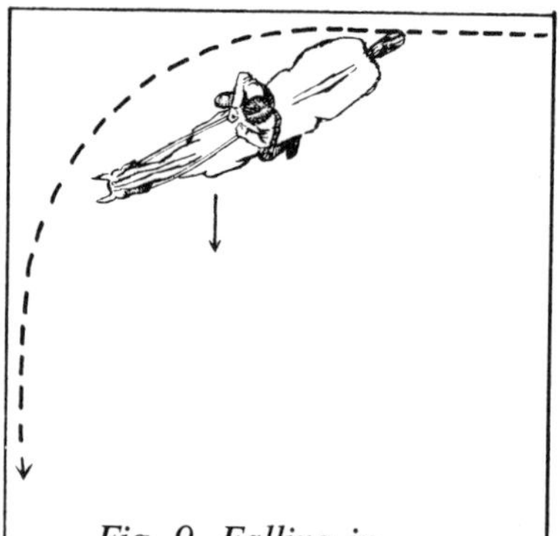

Fig. 9. Falling in

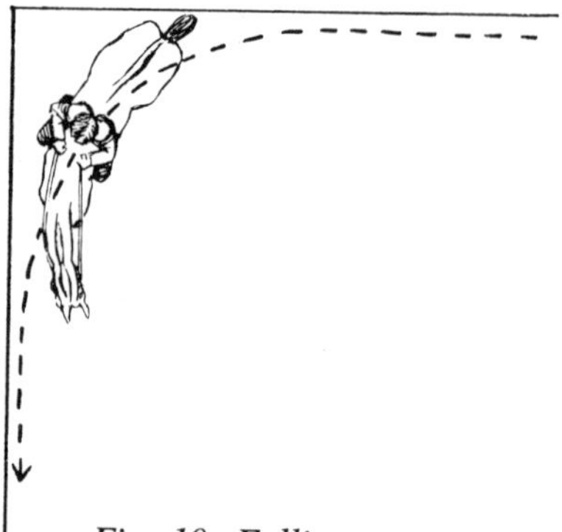

Fig. 10. Falling out

If a circle is attempted, it will become an ever-decreasing spiral.

This fault must be corrected at the walk first, and later at the trot. Working in a large circle put the whip in the inside hand, to reinforce the inside leg, ask the horse for the bend, (just enough to see the back of the eye will do), and then insist on the horse keeping the bend;

the horse will soon know what is wanted, and continued correct bending will supple the spine; one-sidedness will gradually disappear.

At the same time the rider must avoid too much use of the inside rein; if the neck is pulled round too far to the inside, the quarters will tend to 'fall out' instead of following the front legs.

An aid to this exercise is to put an oil drum or other marker near the corner, thus giving the horse something to avoid; this will correct the tendency to fall in; the marker can be gradually put deeper into the corner as the horse gets more supple.

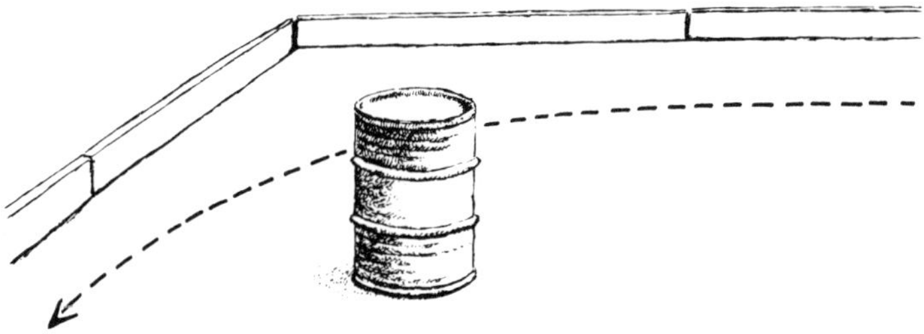

Fig. 11. Marker as an aid to riding the corner

Ride as close to the boards as possible, keeping the horse straight. A bad fault is to allow the horse to carry its 'quarters in'; this fault is especially liable to occur at the canter. It is preferable to ride very slightly 'shoulder-in'—but this is a later refinement, not to be considered yet. At the moment concentrate on absolute straightness.

Fig. 12. Riding with quarters in. A bad fault.

Try and ride straight on the short side as well as the long, as soon as the horse can go into the corner without losing balance.

Your work can be both at sitting and rising trot—remember that at rising trot, when you change the rein you must also 'change the diagonal', i.e. rise and come down on the opposite pair of legs at the trot. If you do not know how to do this, get an instructor to show you. The object is to prevent the horse developing its muscles more on one side than the other.

Next, you may start to teach the horse to go straight up the centre line. This is surprisingly hard to do, and impossible without some sort of guide. Either mow a straight line up the centre, or else put pairs of boards about one yard apart, at D, X, and G.

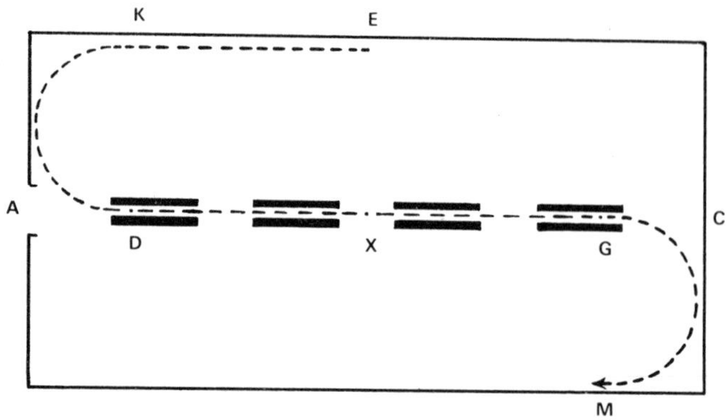

Fig. 13. Aids to riding up the centre line

Riding up the Centre line

On the left rein, approach K from E, and just after K make a perfect half-circle of just under 10 metres diameter; this will take you exactly into the two boards at D; if your horse puts his head down to look at the boards, so much the better. Now fix your eyes on C and ride straight to G, where you can make a half-circle right to M. If you work with boards, your horse will get the habit of going straight. Practise walking as well as trotting, on the centre line, and halting between the boards.

'Overshooting' the centre line is a bad fault, as is 'wandering' or being 'off-line'. All will lose you marks in a test. Do not try to do this exercise at the canter yet, because the half-circle at the end is too small for a novice horse.

Circles

We will now consider the riding of circles.

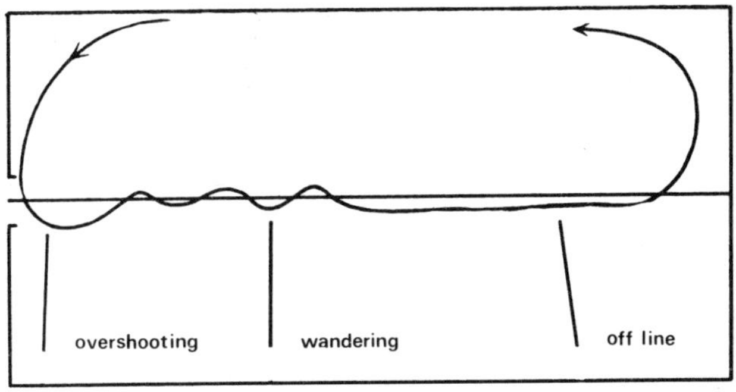

Fig. 14. Faults on the centre line

The circles for novice tests will be of 20 metres—the full width of the arena. They will start and end either at A or C, B or E. The circles from A and C pass through X, and touch the track 4 metres from the 'diagonal markers'. The circles from B or E touch the track at the opposite marker and cut the centre line exactly half-way between X and the short side. 20 metre circles may be ridden at trot or canter. Note that K, H, M, F, D and G are *not* on any 20 metre circle.

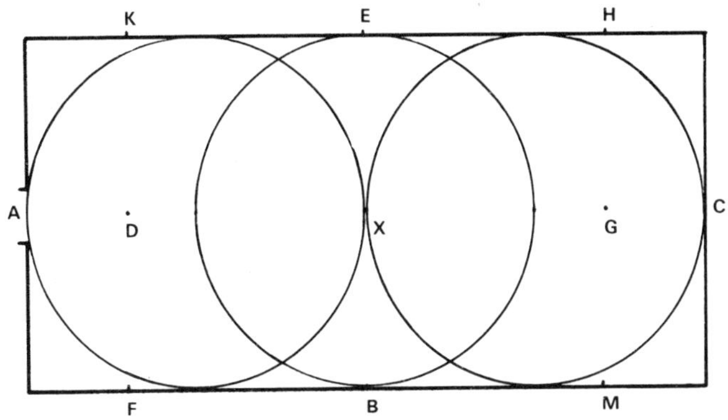

Fig. 15. 20 metre circles in the small arena

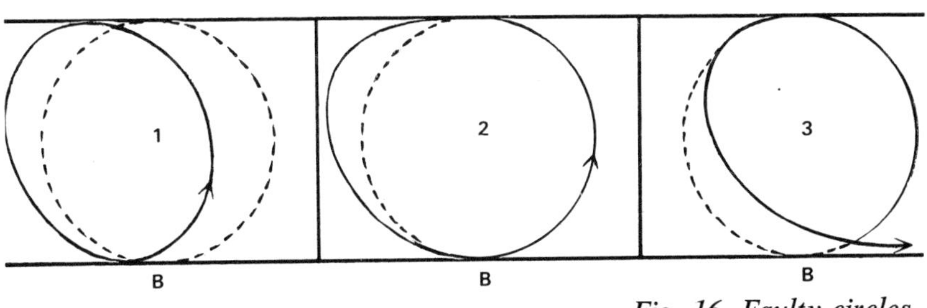

Fig. 16. Faulty circles

"Circle not round"—how often does the judge write this! The main faults are: 1. turning in too sharply off the track at the start of the circle; 2. remaining in the track too long at the opposide side, or 3. "falling-in" towards the end of the circle.

"Circle too small" speaks for itself, and is another common fault. After riding a circle beginning and ending at A or C, remember to go straight on into the corner, rather than making yet another quarter of a circle. (*Fig 17*)

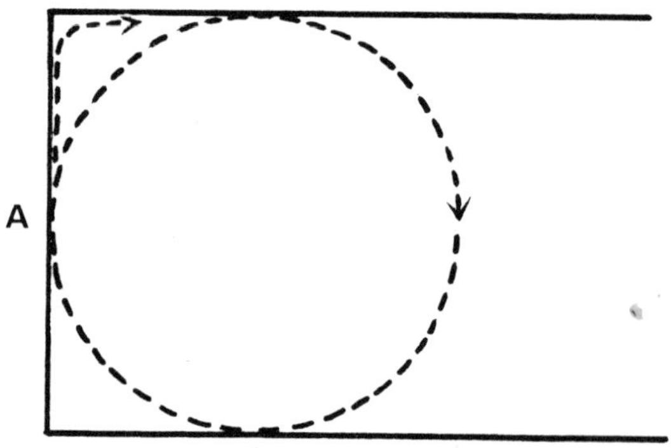

10 metre half-circles may be performed at the walk or trot by novice horses. A 10 metre half circle should end exactly on the centre line facing the end marker. (*Fig 18*)

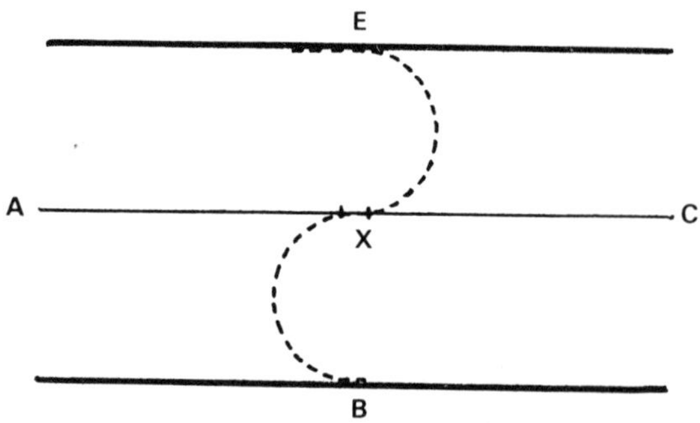

Above: Linked 10 metre half-circles—note that at X the rider takes one or two strides straight *on* the centre line. Remember that the centre line is 10 metres from the long side; circles of 15, 8, 5 metres may be required in later tests.

Serpentines and Loops

These figures are generally shown in diagrams on the back of the test sheet.

The commonest are—

1. Linked half circles of 20 metres, AX-XC. (*Fig 19*)
   Note that at X the rider should face exactly towards B or E, and ride straight on the BE line for a horse's length.

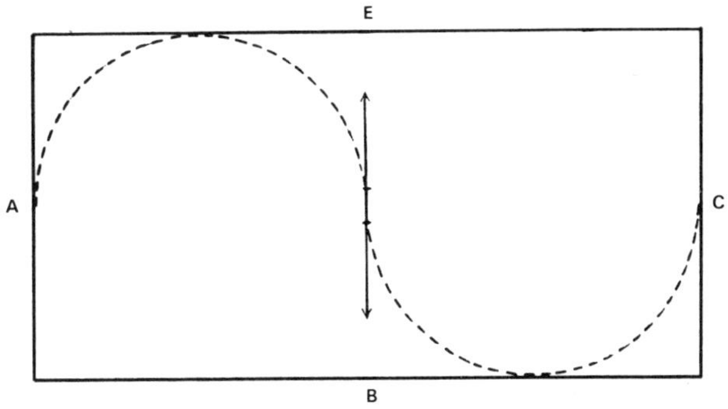

2. Serpentine three loops, A to C. (*Fig 20*)
   A difficult movement. The middle loop meets the track exactly at B, the outer loops half a metre from K and H, and cut the centre line at one-third and two-thirds of the total length. The loops are *not* perfect half-circles. Loops must be exactly equal.

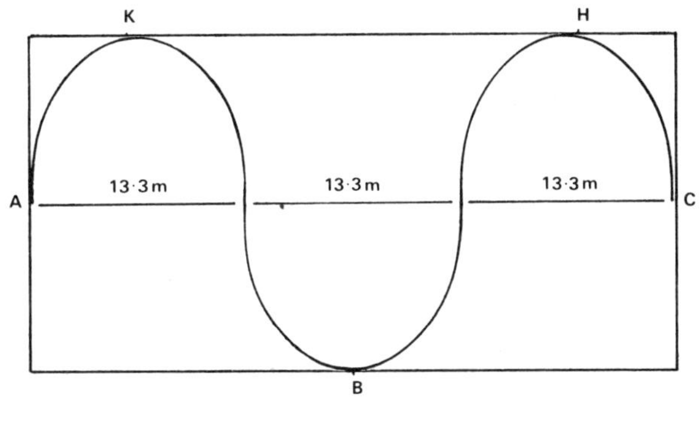

3. Serpentine of three, four or more loops each side of centre line, depth of loops to be given in metres. Loops must be equal. (*Fig 21*)

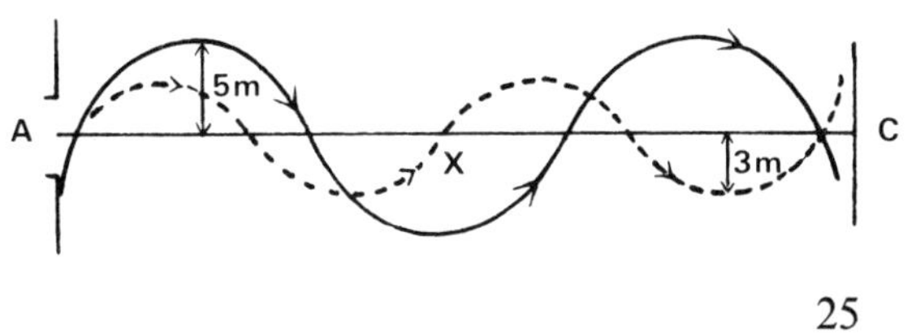

C

4. Loop K to H on long side, depth given in metres. (*Fig 22*)

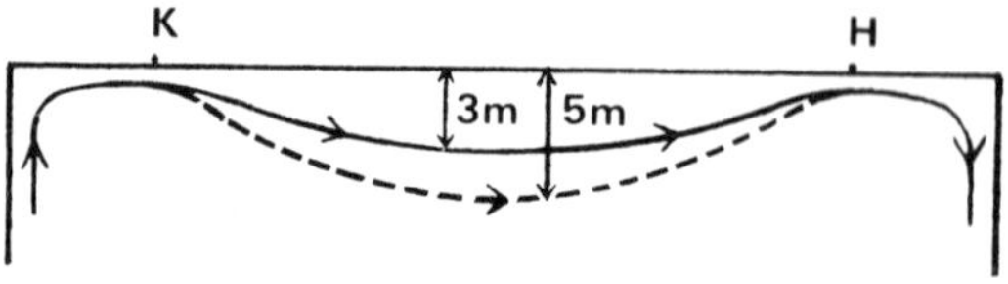

These last serpentines are ridden without changing leg at the canter. The horse must keep the bend over the leading leg.

Serpentines and loops must be ridden with meticulous attention to the correct bend; the rider must keep the horse balanced when changing rein, and "change the diagonal" if at rising trot. There must be no loss of rhythm, nor change of speed. One must get the impression that the horse having accepted the correct bend from hand, seat and leg aids, will then continue indefinitely in that curve until the aids are changed.

Riding in a curve with the wrong bend is a very bad fault, and will ensure that in a test the marks will be no better than insufficient. From the point of view of schooling the horse, allowing a wrong bend is merely failing to take the opportunity to supple the horse, thus permitting it to reinforce a bad habit.

The accurate riding of circles and serpentines is a valuable exercise, since it demands exact placing of the horse by the rider—no horse would describe a circle on its own except by chance—the acceptance of the bend has a suppling effect on the neck and back, which leads naturally on to the next phase in the horse's training—the horse accepting the bit, with flexion at the poll, and correct engagement of the hocks.

Riding in the arena creates a 'sense of space' in the horse; it will soon start to accept the boundaries and to be content to remain within them. The rider will find that it is much easier to relax a fresh horse, and thus to concentrate on the work in hand.

Chapter 4

Impulsion

The power unit of the horse is in the hind quarters. When on the move, the front legs, like spokes of the wheel of a wheelbarrow, support much of the weight, while the propulsion comes from behind.

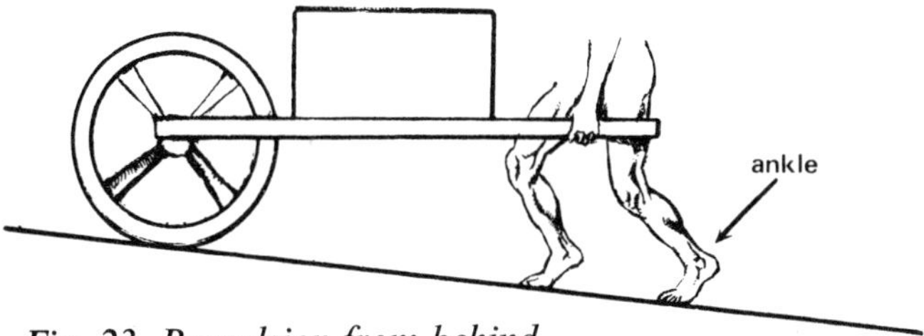

Fig. 23. Propulsion from behind

The ankle joint of the human being is the hock joint of the horse, the human toes being fused together in the foot of the horse. (In the human arm, the wrist is the equivalent of the horse's knee).

Fig. 24. The hind leg

Our general definition spoke of "lightening of the forehand and engagement of the hind quarters". If our man with the barrow wanted to lift the front wheel off the ground, he plainly could not do it by holding the extreme end of the shafts; he would move forward as far as he could and get his legs as much under the barrow as possible,

Fig. 25. Lightening the forehand

crouching down to get as much leverage as possible from his back muscles.

So with the horse, when we wish to lighten the forehand we must 'engage' the hocks by bringing them under the body; the further they are brought under, the more weight can the hind legs support, until in the extreme case, the *levade*, the whole weight is taken upon the hind legs, with the hocks flexed and the quarters lowered to half their normal height from the ground.

Fig. 26. Engaging the quarters

Try this experiment: get down on all fours with hands well stretched out in front of you. Now try to lift both hands at once from the floor without swaying back; it is impossible, until you bring your knees gradually forward under your body. Your hands will gradually become lighter, and at a critical moment it will become possible to lift them. A minute adjustment of balance the other way, and down they will go again. When you reach the critical point, try the effect on the balance of raising or lowering the head and leaning forward or back.

This is what is meant by the phrases 'hocks out behind', 'horse going on the forehand' (i.e. too much weight on the forehand); 'hocks not engaged'. Naturally the picture is more complicated when the horse is moving. The action of bringing the hocks under the horse, thus shortening his 'wheelbase', is the most important part of the process known as 'collecting the horse'. In addition the weight on the forehand can be reduced by shortening and raising the horse's neck, thus 'collecting' him at both ends.

There is no better illustration of this principle than Müseler's famous diagram, which he calls the "Principle of Collection and Erection". Modern translators would prefer the term "Collection and Elevation"!

The series of pictures below is an adaptation of his drawing.

Fig. 27.

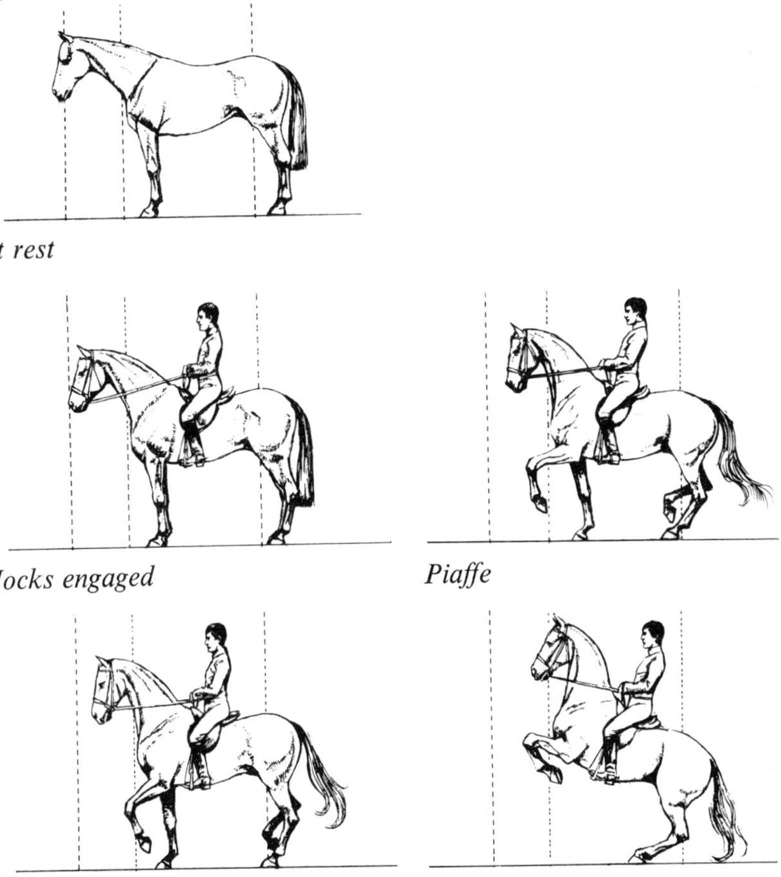

At rest

Hocks engaged

Piaffe

Collected

Levade

Collection and Elevation

Note how, as collection is increased, the hocks are brought further under the body, and flexed to lower the quarters. The neck is shortened and raised, until eventually the forehand leaves the ground.

The effect of shortening the neck is automatically to shorten the stride of the front legs—some consider that a horse cannot put his fore foot *on the ground* further than a point vertically below his nose (though he can, however, extend it in the air).

The effect of lowering the quarters and flexing the hock is to give bounce and elevation—known as 'cadence'—to the stride. Thus we see that at collected paces the horse will take a shorter and more elevated stride, though it can, and should, maintain the same rhythm.

Fig. 28.

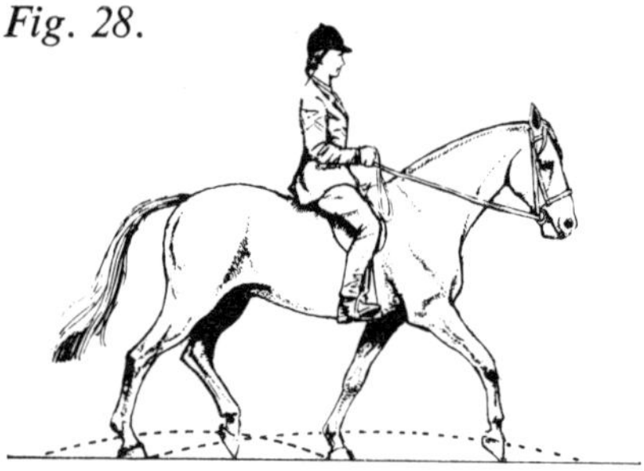

Working trot

Collected trot

Passage

The other effect of collection is to store energy within the frame of the horse, exactly in the same way that energy is contained in a compressed spring. The rider then has the power to release this energy for an extra effort, such as the extended trot, a jump, sudden acceleration, or even such 'airs above the ground' as the *capriole.*

Now for a word of warning—collection imposes a great strain on the muscular system of the horse—*and it cannot be achieved until the proper muscles have been developed.* Look back at the requirements of different standards of dressage, and observe that collection is not required until the Advanced Elementary test—when the horse is nearly ready for Medium work. *It is not for the Novice horse, nor for the novice rider.*

The degree of collection attainable depends on the muscular and mental development of the horse. The novice rider should aim at nothing more than a good 'working trot' in which, according to the F.E.I. definition, the horse shows itself "properly balanced, and with supple poll, remaining on the bit, goes forward with even elastic steps and good hock action."

The aim in the early stages of dressage is to restore the natural grace and balance of the horse, which we have partially paralysed by putting the tremendous weight of a rider and saddle on his back. Have you ever tried to ski or skate with a 30lb rucksack on your back?—it destroys all pleasure in the sport until you have practised for a very long time.

Turn a common horse loose in a field with its companion and watch them float about like thoroughbreds in extended trot and even *passage*, in total contrast to the plodding dullness of their paces when you are on their backs. Yet it is possible to regain this freedom, by correct training.

Collection at the trot

Note how, as collection is increased, the stride becomes shorter and lighter, while the horse's neck is flexed more and slightly raised.

Our efforts to 'engage the hocks' and 'lighten the forehand' will therefore not be devoted to collecting and shortening the horse, but to increasing the power coming from the hind-quarters of the horse, and to lengthening the stride of the forelegs by extending the horse's neck, and by improving the movement of the shoulder. The horse's shoulder is not a solid joint—the shoulder blade is plastered to the rib-cage by muscle and fibre, and therefore its movement, by proper work, can be improved.

We now have the key to the correct attitude for the novice horse, the goal towards which we must work.

First, active hocks, brought well forward under the body.

If the power unit is working well, and the horse is relaxed the pelvis will rotate slightly, giving what is called a 'swinging back'. This will be shown in the movement of the tail, the end of which will swing like a tassel, at the walk and trot.

Fig. 29. The leading leg is brought well forward under the body. The sole of the trailing foot should only be visible for an instant

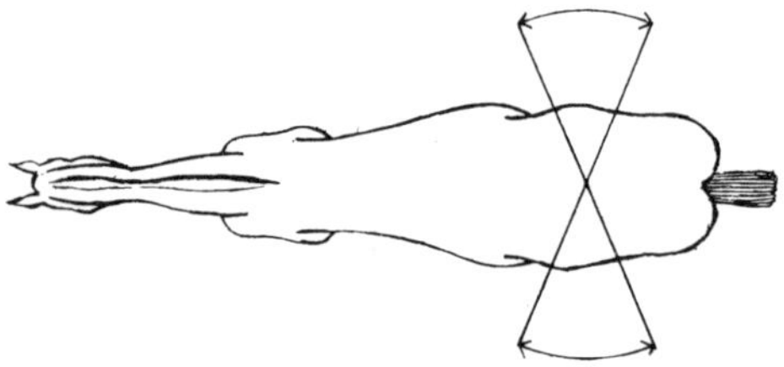

Fig. 30. A swinging back

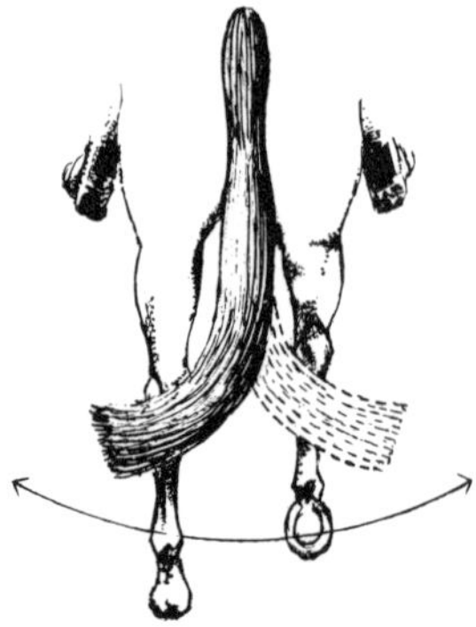

Fig. 31. Action of the tail, showing a swinging back

Second—a long neck, with the face slightly in front of the vertical.

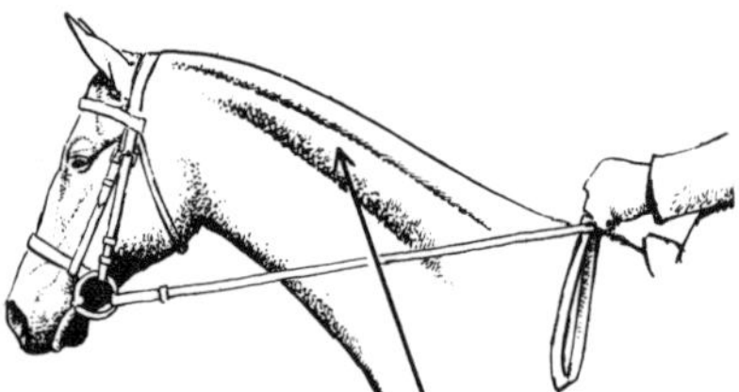

Fig. 32. Attitude and action of the neck. A good attitude for a novice horse; when the horse is going well, the muscle arrowed will be prominent, and will be seen to contract and expand in time with the stride

The problem for the beginner will be how to persuade the horse to carry his head in the correct position. The young unbroken horse will very often have a natural head carriage, and will soon adopt the right attitude; but the 'spoilt' horse will have developed wrong habits and wrong muscles.

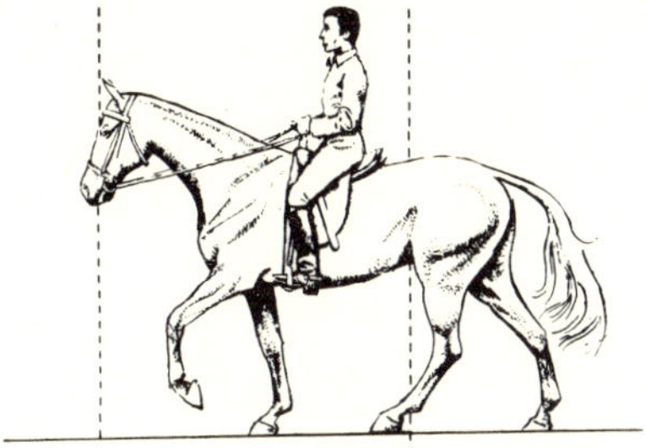

Fig. 33 (a). The whole relaxed, yet lively and active

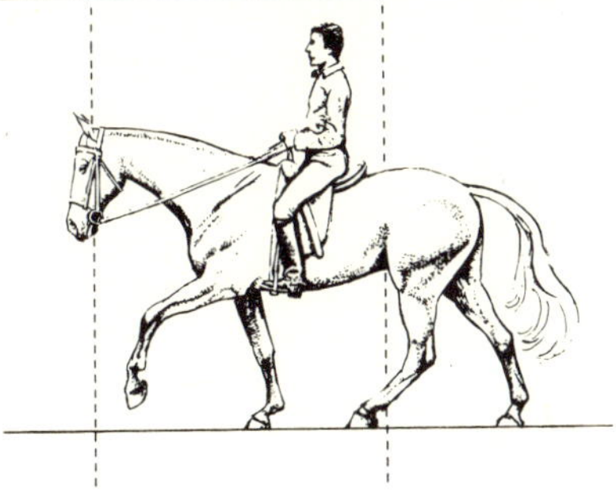

Fig. 33 (b) When asked for extended pace, the neck should go slightly out and down

Some common faults illustrated.

Fig. 34. Above the bit, rider trying vainly to pull horse's head down. Legs pushed forward in the stirrups accentuate the tendency of horse to pull against the rider.

Fig. 35. Overbent, pulling, horse leaning on the bit.

Fig. 36. Ewe neck, hollow back, stride very cramped, horse tending to "trample" up and down, rather than going forward.

Fig. 37. Behind the bit (or over the bit), attitude similar to overbending, but the horse drops the bit intermittently, and the reins go slack.

Fig. 38. Running, the horse pokes its nose, kicks the soles of the hind feet out backwards, and hurries; all the weight is on the forehand. Produced in a mistaken attempt to lengthen the stride at the trot.

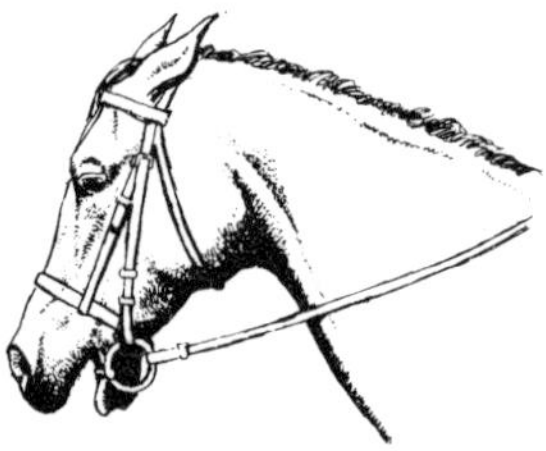

Fig. 39. Broken neck, flexion too far behind the poll. Though so-called, it has little to do with dislocated vertebrae, but is a wrongly developed muscular formation, caused by forcing the horse into flexion too early in its training. Fig. 40. Mouth open, shows lack of relaxation, and non-acceptance of the bit. Ears laid back, unwillingness or resistance. In this case, the bit is too low in the horses mouth, causing discomfort. Fig. 41. Tongue protruding, the tongue has probably got over the bit—a bad fault, and difficult to cure; generally caused by rough hands in the early stages. If the tongue is protruded for short periods, without being over the bit, the fault is not so serious. The trouble may be due to insufficient room for the tongue under the bit.

Fig. 42. Tilted head, horse resisting on one side, often caused by faulty teeth; or by the hand influence being stronger than that of the seat and leg. Crossing the jaw. The lower jaw is pushed sideways, a certain sign of resistance.

Fig. 43. Wide behind, generally caused by pushing the horse beyond its capabilities in an effort to lengthen the stride at the trot. Young racehorses often gallop wide behind, through being asked to gallop before the canter is properly established.

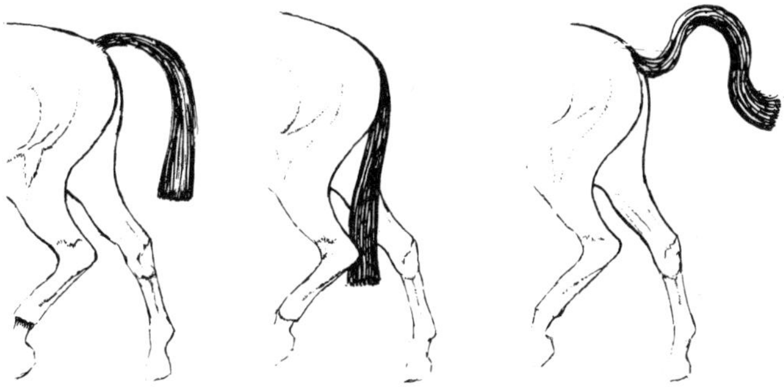

Fig. 44. Tail high—often goes with 'hollow back'. Some breeds, notably Arab, have high tail carriage as a natural characteristic. Fig. 45. Tail tucked-in and dead—lack of energy. Fig. 46. Tail swishing—resistance.

Fig. 47. Croup high, a horse with stiff hock action at the canter, carries its croup high, and appears to be cantering down hill, instead of flexing the hocks and lowering the quarters.

Fig. 48 (a), 48 (b). Four-time canter. The sequence of footfalls for a horse cantering, as below, near fore leading, is: off-hind, right diagonal, near-fore, giving a beat of one-two-three. If the horse loses balance, the rhythm breaks up, and the two feet of the diagonal do not strike the ground simultaneously, thus producing four beats.

Note this illustration does not show the fault, only the moment at which both legs of the right diagonal are coming to the ground.

The art of getting a horse to flex correctly is not easily learnt; the first thing to realise is that it is not done by the hands. You can sit all day on a horse, trying to pull the head down with the reins, and the horse will merely pull back at you—this will make things worse, since you are exercising the 'pulling' muscles and developing them still further. Flexion comes from behind, and can be produced by the rider's leg. Try the experiment of halting the horse; take a steady but light contact on both reins *without pulling*. Now gently fold your legs round the horse with soft inward (not backward) impulses. If the horse tries to move forward restrain him with the reins and use the legs less strongly; gradually he will start to dip his head lower. When he does so, reward him by encouragement by voice, a pat, and lightening the contact.

If he tries to snatch the rein from you, hold firm, but do not pull—let the horse feel he himself is making the discomfort by coming up against an unyielding bit.

Although this is not the correct way of getting true flexion—since it is done at the halt and not on the move—it will show you that flexion comes from a steady hand, accepting and controlling the impulse from the leg. Any unsteadiness of hand will cause movement of the bit in the horse's mouth, which will at once cause him to lift his head. Try shaking a rein, if the horse's head is too low, and the effect will be to raise the head at once.

Our aim must now be to get the horse to extend his head and neck forward and downward—no matter if it is too low at first provided that rhythm and tempo are maintained. The sequence of training so far has therefore been—

1. Relax the horse, and allow him to find his rhythm.
2. Get free forward movement—straight.
3. Teach the horse to bend on curves.
4. Persuade him to lower his head and extend the neck, 'looking for the bit'.
5. Increase the power from behind, and the engagement of the hocks, to lighten the forehand.

Lastly, we must train him to maintain this attitude at all times—especially during changes of direction, and transitions from one pace to another.

This can only be achieved by the most delicate balance on the part of the rider, who must sit still, neither bumping the horse's back, nor wobbling sideways, nor back and forwards. The rider's spine must be as carefully balanced in the vertical plane as a pile of wooden bricks, his hands must be as steady as though holding two glasses of water, his legs softly encouraging the forward movement. Hence the importance of a correct seat, which 'follows' the horse's movement, and keeps the rider's balance over the horse's centre of gravity.

If you find yourself bumping at the sitting trot, try holding the front arch of the saddle, and pulling yourself down into it. At once the bumping will decrease—you will be 'going with the horse' instead of against it, and it is this harmonious contact between horse and rider which is the essence of good riding. A horse with hocks engaged, and back swinging, will be far more comfortable to sit on, than one with a high head and hollow back, on which the rider will feel as though sitting on a board.

Naturally, the path to success will not be smooth: the horse will find innumerable resistances, some of which will seem impossible to overcome. The rider can only seek expert advice; a knowledgeable person can often see at once what is causing the resistance—generally a fault on the rider's part—and can help the rider to correct the trouble.

Let us end this chapter, which is headed 'impulsion', with some consideration of this elusive word, which has many meanings for different people. Some just take it to mean 'energy', i.e. 'lacking impulsion' meaning 'lacking energy'; but energy alone is not impulsion—it must be *energy completely under control.* Impulsion does not mean 'speed'—a horse may run fast round the arena, but completely lack impulsion. Colonel Handler* prefers this definition —"a tendency to move forward with elasticity, originating from the haunches, flowing into a swinging back, ending in the mouth".

*Former head of the Spanish Riding School.

Chapter 5

Transitions and halts

A transition is the change from one pace to another; at Novice standard the transitions are mainly performed from one pace to the next—i.e. walk to trot, trot to canter; at Elementary standard, the horse is expected to canter from the walk or vice versa; and at Advanced standard we find transitions from rein-back to canter, extended canter to walk.

If you read any test, and count the number of transitions, you will find them occurring more often than any other movement—e.g. in Test No. 1, there are fourteen, including the two halts.

It follows, therefore, that if the transitions are badly done, there are plenty of opportunities for losing marks.

Transitions are of two kinds—upward, to a higher pace, and downward, to a lower pace. The former are the easier, since the horse is being asked to go forward, whereas in downward transitions it must 'come back' to the rider.

Transitions must be *straight*, no swinging of the quarters, *smooth*, with no loss of balance, *steady* with the horse's head maintained in the correct attitude, *soft*, with no wrangling or resistance, and they must be '*forward*'; that is to say the horse must not be checked, and the *first stride of the new pace must be a full one.*

At Novice standard where a transition is required to be made to the next pace but one—e.g. halt to trot, trot to halt—it may be made progressively—that is to say, with a stride or two of walk intervening between halt and trot.

Upward transitions demand instant response to the leg, in order that the transition is accurate, and that the horse goes immediately into the next pace.

Downward transitions demand the ability to 'engage the hocks' and lighten the forehand, or the horse will lurch forward and pull at the reins.

Our man with the wheelbarrow, if he wishes to apply the brakes on a hill, must put his feet forward under the barrow. So the rider, to

Fig. 49. Putting on the brakes

check the horse, must first ride it a little into the bit, to bring the hocks more underneath the body.

This action, preparatory to a downward transition, is called a 'half-halt'; it should never be obvious to the spectator, but should take place unobtrusively and quietly.

Beginners are often bewildered by the fact that in order to *reduce* speed at the canter on a green horse, it is generally necessary to use the legs quite strongly in order to drive the hocks under the body.

Downward transitions cannot be performed smoothly until we have the ability to 'bring the horse back' to us, by engaging the hocks. Once the horse is going freely forward, bending to right and left, and beginning to flex a little at the poll, we must work towards improving its suppleness in the vertical plane by asking the horse for frequent increase and decrease of speed, engaging the hocks, reducing speed, and then asking for a longer stride once more. This work is better done in the open, rather than in the confines of the arena, where we lack the natural tendency of the horse to go straight forward.

At first the canter is likely to be too fast; when asked to reduce speed, the horse will fall into the trot; but gradually, as balance improves, so will the horse gain in impulsion; then, quite suddenly, the rider will find that he is able to canter calmly and quietly, without difficulty, the horse holding itself in balance.

Once this stage is reached, transitions become comparatively easy. The horse will canter, without effort, from the walk, and will soon be able to walk from the canter.

When working in the arena, the rider must avoid performing transitions regularly in the same place. The horse learns to anticipate transitions more rapidly than any other movement, seeming able to sense the rider's intentions—which are in fact, telegraphed through hand and seat. Many tests are ruined by anticipation—especially in movements where after the walk, the horse is asked to trot or canter. The rider becomes tense, the horse shortens the stride and starts to jog up and down, following with an explosive or crooked strike-off to canter.

The rider, therefore, when working, will do better to concentrate on the smooth execution of the transitions, rather than on the accuracy of their placing, thus not letting the horse anticipate where the transitions are going to be made. In a test, remember that a good transition, early or late, will get better marks, than a bad transition made right on the marker.

There is one movement, however, which does not suffer from anticipation—that is the lengthening of strides across the diagonal of the school at walk or trot. In most tests, the free walk, and the medium trot or extended trot, take place on the diagonal; if the horse acquires the habit of stepping out on that line, no harm will come of it; the rider can always restrain, but cannot always produce a lengthened stride at will. Horses have quite a sense of space and direction, and will soon get into the habit of going a little more strongly as the rider turns on to the diagonal. A discreet click of the tongue, inaudible to the judge, will help matters even further!

The transition to the halt is very often done carelessly at the lower levels of dressage.

The rider must realise that any crookedness, however slight, is liable to severe penalty—most horses tend to swing the quarters to one side in the halt, because the rider has not been careful enough to absorb the energy softly in the mouth. The result is that the quarters continue to try and move forward, when the forehand is stationary; the quarters, having nowhere else to go, must move sideways.

An even more serious fault is fidgetting—the horse *must* remain still with all four feet; stepping back is a particularly bad mistake. Inattention, looking about, or tossing the head up and down is also wrong. Horses must be taught the discipline of standing still when being mounted, while the rider takes up the reins and adjusts stirrups or girth.

Lesser faults include not standing square; being slightly off line; resting a leg; not being on the bit, including the hocks being too far out behind.

The transition from the halt, to walk or trot—generally called the 'move-off', must be absolutely straight.

The halt is best practised while hacking; the rider should, if necessary, halt hundreds of times, until the horse understands clearly what is required.

The third illustration (adapted from Müseler) shows the correct method of riding downward transitions, and the effective use of the rider's back and legs in engaging the hocks.

Fig. 50.
Wrong—rider pulling reins only, without using leg aid. Horse fighting and wrangling into halt.

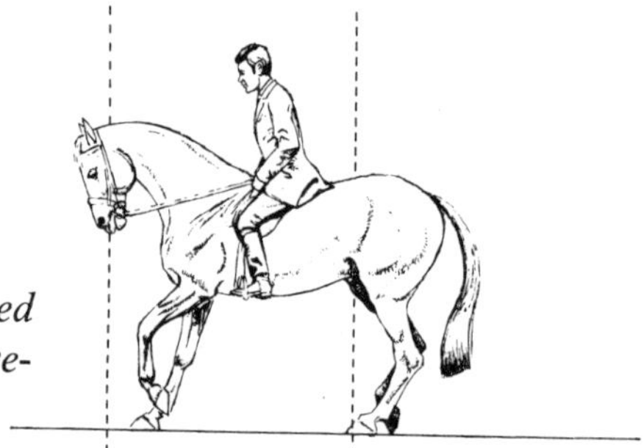

Wrong method of reducing speed —horse pulling up on the forehand, rider's hands too low

Correct downward transition, rider bracing back and using legs to engage hocks horses quarters are lowered

Fig. 51. Off line, crooked, not square, inattentive—very bad
Straight—but not on the bit, resting hind leg—insufficient
On the bit, straight and square, good

The rein-back is not required in Novice Tests, though many trainers include it in their schooling. F.E.I. rules define it thus:—

"The rein-back is a . . . retrograde movement in which the feet are raised and set down almost simultaneously by diagonal pairs; each fore foot being raised and set down an instant before the diagonal hind foot . . . the feet should be well raised and the hind feet remain well in line."

The definition goes on to detail the faults: hurrying, evading the hand, quarters crooked, and so on, ending with the phrase "a horse that is not obedient to the aids of the rider in the rein-back is insufficiently suppled, badly schooled, or badly ridden."

The aids for the rein-back correspond with those for the halt; that is to say the horse is ridden into the bit from behind, engaging the hocks; the reins act persuasively, asking the horse to move backwards, step by step; pulling at the reins without leg pressure is wrong. The horse must keep his head still, and move back without resistance for the exact number of steps required. Relaxation, straightness, and two-time movement are the most important requirements. The horse should flex his hocks and thus lower his quarters. If the hocks are not flexed, the movement will throw weight on the forehand, and the horse will shuffle his forefeet along the ground.

The rein-back is valuable, not only as an exercise to lighten the forehand, but also as an indication of progress in the training of the novice. Any stiffness in the back, wrangling or resistance in the mouth, or lack of ability to engage the hocks, will immediately be apparent.

The rein-back is normally followed by a forward movement, the first stride of which must be a full one straight into the required pace, without a progressive transition.

Chapter 6

Through the judge's eyes

The judge of a dressage competition has the task of sorting as many as thirty or more competitors into an order of merit—in pure dressage the order is more important than the marks, but in Combined Training the marks are carried forward towards the aggregate total.

With such large numbers, the judge cannot rely on comparison, since many hours may elapse between the first and last starters; the judge must use absolute standards, comparing each candidate with the ideal. Naturally, the higher the standard, the fewer the faults; and at top levels the judge may penalise almost invisible errors which would be condoned in the lower standards.

A test consists of a number of movements, each marked out of 10, each mark signifying a standard. The scale is as follows:

10 excellent	5 sufficient
9 very good	4 insufficient
8 good	3 fairly bad
7 fairly good	2 bad
6 satisfactory	1 very bad
	0 not performed

(There is also a scale, out of 6, used in some tests, e.g. at Badminton —6 very good, 5 good, 4 fairly good, 3 passable, 2 bad, 1 very bad 0 not performed.)

At the end of the test there are one or more headings for marks for general impression of the horse, and a final heading for marks for the position and seat of the rider, and correct application of the aids.

The marks are totalled, penalties being deducted for losing the way, using the voice, or (in some tests) going over the time allowed; from all this the final score emerges. In advanced tests some movements of particular importance are multiplied by a coefficient of 2x or 3x.

Beside each movement on the sheet is a space in which the judge can make remarks, justifying the mark; at the end the judge also remarks on the general impression of the horse and rider.

Riders sometimes complain when judges make a mark without comment; but they should remember that a mark represents a statement—"insufficient", "fairly bad"; further explanation may not be necessary.

The judge must have a writer, to whom marks and remarks are dictated.

There are therefore three ways in which horse and rider can gain or lose marks.

1. What the horse *is*—i.e., its paces, movement, carriage, suppleness, attitude, lightness, energy, muscular development—as shown in the basic paces, its acceptance of the bit, and of the rider's weight and aids.
2. What the horse *does*, i.e., how well each movement is performed, and whether it is performed in exactly the right place.
3. What the rider is and does.

The first element is the most important—and will set the general standard throughout the test; — that is, if the basic paces are faulty, the horse *must* receive low marks, however accurately it may go through the movements. Conversely a horse is unlikely to get marks of "excellent" or "very good" standard, unless its general movement is also of this quality—and a horse of this standard is rare.

In the detailed movements the judge will be looking to see that the horse maintains the correct footfall and rhythm through the movement, that it maintains its attitude through the transitions, and that it performs the movements not only according to the requirements laid down in the rules, but also at the right place. When a movement has to be performed at a certain point, it is when the rider's body is above that point that the movement should be executed.

In the third element, that of the rider, the judge will look for faults of position, and exaggerated or wrong application of the aids. It is not always easy to allot these marks, especially when one is judging a good rider on a horse that is going badly, or when a rider, by apparently inelegant methods, is getting very good results.

Major faults will result in the loss of at least two or more marks—such faults being incorrect paces, uneven rhythm, unlevel paces, horse crooked, pulling, wrongly bent or stiff, tongue over the bit, overbent, above bit, etc.

Lesser faults vary with the stage of training, but include unsteady head, bucking, putting out the tongue, momentary loss of balance, inaccuracy, slight resistance, and so on.

The judge must look for the good as well as for the bad, must include praise as well as criticism, and, without attempting to act as a trainer, try and contribute something which will be helpful to the competitor.

The judge must be impartial, ignoring previous performances or knowledge of the horse, favouritism or prejudice for or against the rider.

There are other pressures too—the time-table, fatigue, and sometimes the presence of another judge who may be more cautious in the allotment of marks. Some judges are afraid to give very high or very low marks; when good competitors appear they become 'crabby' and mark them down, and when bad riders come in, they feel sorry for them and are afraid of hurting their feelings. Judges must have the courage of their convictions, reward merit generously, and condemn the bad unmercilessly. The medicine can be sweetened by kind remarks at the end.

Competitors should not be afraid to consult the judge after the competition, if they do not understand any remark; the judge's duty is to help the competitor.

All judges are different; and judging dressage is a matter of opinion and not of fact. Three judges, sitting at different viewpoints, may see the same movement in quite different ways, and give varying marks. Some faults may go unnoticed by one judge, or may not weigh so heavily with him. In all sport, the competitors must submit themselves to the judge—and accept the verdict in a good spirit. If the competitor thinks a particular judge is wrong, there is nothing to be done about it; but if a competitor begins to think that every judge is wrong, then it is time he looked into the mirror and examined himself!

Chapter 7

Riding a test

Before taking part in a competition, the rider must get a schedule from the Secretary of the event. This document will tell the conditions for entry, the qualifications necessary, the time and place of the show, the date of the closing of entries, the time by which final declarations must be made, and a telephone number from which the competitor can ascertain the starting time on the evening before the show. Study the schedule carefully, and note the details in your diary; a late entry may not be accepted, and failure to declare may involve loss of the entry fee.

Next, get a copy of the Test to be ridden (from the British Horse Society, National Equestrian Centre, Stoneleigh, Kenilworth, Warwickshire) and then learn the test thoroughly by heart—but *not* by repeating it on the horse on which you are going to compete. It is essential to know the test really well, because if something goes wrong, and you lose your concentration, you will find that the next movement has gone out of your mind completely.

When laying out your arena at home, remember that the judges are normally placed with their backs to the sun; if you are accustomed to orientate yourself in this way, it may prevent confusion when you arrive at a strange arena.

Now you may practise the movements of the test, but do not on any account repeat the test in the correct sequence more than a very few times, or your horse will start to anticipate the next movement—once this happens, it is very difficult to cure; it is better to perform the movements separately, as part of your programme of work, only fitting them together as a final check that you know the sequence correctly.

If your memory is bad, or if you are riding several different tests, then it may be wise to have a 'commander' who will read the test out loud to you. This is not allowed in Combined Training, nor in F.E.I. tests.

When the day comes, arrive at the ground in plenty of time to 'ride in', to get your horse accustomed to the strange place, and to get rid of any freshness or high spirits which may spoil the test. Report to the Secretary and collect your number; 'ride in', wearing your comfortable clothes, and put on your best kit at the last moment. Spurs are optional at Novice standard.

Watch another competitor or two before your own turn.

The steward will warn you when your time is coming; walk quietly round in the collecting area when the previous competitor is performing, and as soon as he finishes, go and ride round the outside of the arena, showing your horse the boards, the letters, and judge's car, all of which may look different from the familiar arena at home.

When the judge is ready she (in this case) will signal, by horn, bell or whistle, and you must then go, without delay, to A, and prepare to enter and start the test.

We will take you through Test Number 4; Preliminary Standard, on your cob, Conker, at his and your first appearance in public.

1. A **Enter at working trot**—straight up the centre line—which to your horror, is painted in a brilliant white, unlike the mown line at home—Conker will not go within two feet of it.

   X **Halt—salute—move off at working trot rising.** The halt is straight, but you can feel through your seat that the quarters are not level, so Conker is (as usual) resting a hind leg. Now—salute—reins in left hand—hat off (man) or bow (lady)—take the reins, and off goes Conker before you are ready; never mind, hope the judge didn't notice!

   Judge's thoughts This combination looks quite businesslike, but the horse is obviously a bit green. The trot is satisfactory, without being in any way brilliant or spectacular.

   Judge's comment "*Entry off line—halt not square—and not sustained*"—4

2. C **Track to right.** This is the first corner, at all costs show a proper bend. Conker is eyeing the judge's car, ready to shy off and "fall in" round the corner. Remember the inside leg, ease the outside rein, and you are round quite well.

   B **Sitting trot, circle right 20 metres diameter. On returning to B,**

rising trot. Keep up the speed and the rhythm, don't let Conker hold back under your weight. On reaching the white line, Conker jumps it, but, fortunately, does not break into a canter. On crossing it again he eyes it suspiciously, and behaves as though it was a *cavaletti*.

Judge's thoughts—The rider is making a good effort to maintain the correct bends, and the horse is going forward quite willingly, though we shall have to take a mark off for jumping the white line.

Judge's comment—"*Trot rhythm good*"—5.

3. A **Turn down centre.**

C **Track to left.** Make a half circle on to this confounded white line again—is it better to try and make Conker stay on it, or go straight up beside it? Try and get as close to it as possible, stay straight, and ride *forward* as firmly as possible. Conker settles for a path a foot to the right, and then goes straight and well. Don't forget to change diagonals after X, and prepare for the bend to the left at C.

Judge's thoughts—Rider sensibly chose to go slightly off line (which must be penalised).

Judge's comment—"*Off line but straight*"—5.

4. E **Sitting trot, circle left 20 metres diameter.** No excitements this time, Conker has now come to terms with the white line.

Judge's thoughts–Quite a nice round circle, the horse has good rhythm, but the trot is rather limited by the "cobby" conformation of the hourse.

Judge's comment—*nil*—mark 6.

5. K **Working canter left.** Coming out of the circle, you have to canter before the corner at K, just where you leave the track to round the corner. Conker has now gone rather dead, and at the first application of the aid, nothing happens, so a second and more violent kick sends him hastily into a rather scrambling canter.

A **Circle left 20 metres.** He is now going rather too fast, so by the time he has reached X in the circle you are struggling to get back to A.

Judge's thoughts—The greenness is showing now—a disobedience to the aid at the strike-off, and then too fast and on the forehand in the canter, lost her direction in the circle—three bad mistakes —one can't say the whole movement is anything but "bad". We will watch for the transition to trot, and it is pretty certain that the horse will either fall on to the forehand, or flop back into the trot of his own accord.

Judge's comment—"*Rough strike off—canter unbalanced—circle not round*"—2

6. F **Working canter**

K **Working trot sitting.** The main thing now is to try and steady Conker to a more reasonable speed, round the arena, and to prepare him for the transition to the trot at K. Unfortunately, you overdo the "half-halt" in trying to collect him before K, and he slumps into the trot at E.

Judge's thoughts—As I expected.

Judge's comment—"*Canter on forehand—fell into trot early*"—3

7. A **Medium walk.**

BX **Half circle left 10 metres diameter**

XE **Half circle right 10 metres diameter.** Prepare in plenty of time for transition to the walk at A, now walk on briskly, go into the corner and show a nice bend; at B ride forward in a true half circle. A large white blob at X is coming up, so be cunning and switch into the opposite half circle before getting quite on to it (in case Conker decides to shy off it), remember also that he is liable to try to anticipate the trot at E, so interrupt his train of thought by a slight movement of the bit.

Judge's thoughts—The horse walks really well. I think the rider was being cunning, avoiding the white paint at X, which has made the figure a bit misshapen. Rider got a bit tense just before the trot.

Judge's comment—"*Good walk—half-circles not quite even*"—6

8. E **Working trot sitting**

H **Canter right**

C **Circle 20 metres diameter.** Sit down and prepare for the canter; Conker eyes a steward carrying the judge's coffee rather near to the arena, gets the wrong bend at H, and strikes off on the wrong leg! Check him at once, and strike off again correctly this time, but by now you are well round the corner, on the way up the opposite long side—TING—the judge's bell—wrong course!—pull up, look at the judge who has opened her window and is beckoning to you. "Circle at C"—"thank you, I'm so sorry",—back to E, strike off again, Conker circles this time quite well.

Judge's thoughts—The horse was watching that steward—but should not have been so inattentive, and the rider was not really dominating the horse at that point; corrected the wrong strike-off very promptly, and didn't lose her head afterwards, but one can't give more than 4 with a wrong strike-off. Canter is much better balanced this time.

Judge's comment—"*Wrong strike-off, corrected—circle good (after wrong course)*"—4.

9. M **Working canter**

H **Working trot sitting.** Conker is now cantering quietly, and the transition to trot is not bad at all.

Mark—6

10. C **Ordinary walk**

MK **Free walk on long rein**

Conker's favourite movement; but there is a danger point, approaching K, we have got to take up the reins, and trot at K. Conker rather resents coming back on to the bit after the free walk, so if we take the reins too soon, he may throw up his head, and there will be an unseemly wrangle. But if we wait too long, we may not get a good bend in the corner; compromise therefore, and be very tactful taking the reins. Up goes his head, but comes down again almost at once.

Judge's thoughts—The horse really walks well—almost worth an 8, but we will wait and see how well it accepts the taking of the reins before the transition to the trot—some resistance there, so we will drop one mark.

Judge's comment—"*Good free walk—head up in transition*"—7.

11. K **Working trot rising**

A **Turn down centre**

G **Halt, salute, leave arena at free walk**

Make a half circle K to the centre line; put Conker squarely on it this time. He goes well, but swerves round the large white blob at X. He halts square, and straight, but then looks round as if for applause. Salute, smile at the judge, take reins, walk forward, before turning left or right and walking out on a free rein through the exit at A.

Judge's thoughts—Pity she allowed him to look about in the halt, which was otherwise quite nice.

Judge's comments—"*Shied at X—good halt—but inattentive*"—5.

Competitor's thoughts—Well, for a first test it might have been worse; there were no major disasters other than one wrong strike-off to the canter, and that clown Conker treating the white line as if it was a river.

Judge's thoughts—The horse has quite good paces—cobs often do go well 'from behind'; but there was too much shying and swerving, and the canter work was pretty ragged. I don't feel I can give more than 4 at present, though it could easily get a 6 or 7 when it settles better.

When the rider has the horse completely under control, it could do quite a reasonable test.

12. **General impression, smoothness and correct paces of the horse**

"*Horse has quite nice natural paces, canter rather unbalanced at present, but seemed too fresh and inattentive, shying and jumping lines*"—4.

13. **Position and seat of rider, correct application of the aids.**

"*Rider used arena well, horse not always supple in corners, but was correctly bent in circles. Rider does not always keep horse balanced between hand and leg, tending to lose contact, especially at the canter*"—5.

Total	62
Deduct for wrong course	2
	—
	60

The winner got 93, and the worst mark was 41. Conker has an average of less than 5 per movement, so the result was less than "sufficient" at present. But remember that performance in public and in private at home is a very different matter. Both rider and horse will be tense and nervous, and lapses of concentration may occur. By next time, Conker must be made staunch to white lines, and you must work hard to get his hocks more under him, so that he can canter a little slower. The judge liked his paces, and his walk, most difficult to improve, got the highest mark of the test. Many horses which can trot and canter well, show a bad walk, so there is promise of better marks to come.

Work hard and constructively, and remember that "the amateur practises until he can do it right—the professional practises until he cannot do it wrong".

Chapter 8

Conclusion

It is hoped that this book will have given the rider some idea of what the requirements of '*dressage*' are. It has always been a matter of regret that we have no English equivalent for the French word; to complicate the matter further, what has been described in this book is called '*dēbourrage*' by the French—a word with several meanings, including drawing the charge from a loaded musket, and polishing a young gentleman's manners!

There has long been a feeling, which still exists in this country that the whole business is nasty foreign trickery, calculated to "ruin a horse for hunting". Doubtless it would do so for the rider who hangs on by the reins, since any horse with a good mouth will soon stop jumping for the rider who sits back, gets left behind over every fence, and hits the horse in the mouth with the hands.

However, the members of the show-jumping fraternity have fully realised the importance of "work on the flat", the term which they prefer to employ. No one nowadays can win consistently against the clock over big fences with a horse which is not supple, active, well-balanced, and submissive to the rider.

The racing world stands rather aloof from dressage, though some enlightened trainers send horses with severe faults to be cured by dressage riders, and there are examples of notable and consistent successes in the National Hunt world by owners who have adopted simple dressage methods in the early training of steeplechasers, before the young horses have been put into the hands of the trainer. From the riding point of view a scheme for general riding instruction for apprentice jockeys, has been well received by trainers.

Dressage in Great Britain is in a healthy state, thanks to the efforts of the Dressage Committee of the British Horse Society. The panel of judges is now selected, graded, and upgraded by examination; all judges are required to attend one or more annual conferences, to keep in touch with current thought, and new rules. Failure to attend invites removal from the panel. These conferences, often open to riders as well as judges, do much to ensure that all judges are thinking on the same lines.

The beginner—or in fact any dressage rider—should try to attend one of these conferences, or to go and watch experienced instructors at work with their pupils, or to 'sit in' with a judge at a test. Permission to do this is nearly always willingly granted, and will not only help the rider to know the requirements, but also to understand the problems of the judge. With three or four hours consecutive judging, demanding continual concentration, the judge has to make hundreds of rapid decisions, allot a mark, and make a remark, in justification for not giving full marks for the movement. The fact that the 'remarks column' often contains more criticism than praise should not be taken as a personal insult by the rider, but is merely a reflection of the main problem with which the judge is faced—lack of time for anything but the essentials.

This book does not attempt to teach the rider how to ride. As said before, this end cannot be achieved by reading—there is no substitute for good, professional instruction. We cannot teach ourselves to play tennis or golf, to ski or to swim, by the light of nature, without acquiring a fumbling and inefficient technique. The shortest cut to success in acquiring a skill is to learn a sound method, distilled from generations of experience. Wrongly taught faults are desperately hard to eradicate—it is better never to acquire them.

So, if parents want their children to ride well, then let them pay for the best instruction that they can afford. Pony Club membership is within the range of all pockets. For the older rider, membership of a Riding Club may bring the opportunity for professional instruction which would otherwise be too expensive.

Any rider interested in dressage should join the British Horse Society's Dressage Group, which will give access to competitions, conferences, and the Rule Book.

From day to day, the rider must compose his own programme of work. At first the beginner may find it hard to "think of things to do". A regular lesson, say once a fortnight, from an experienced rider or teacher, will ensure that the rider is given something on which to work until the next lesson—the cure of a tendency to stiffness on one side, the improvement of response to the leg aid, '*cavaletti*' work to increase the flexion of the hocks, and so on. The rider will soon be able to use the arena, or the daily exercise ride, to the best advantage.

The great pleasure in dressage is that the rider becomes conscious that, in every step that the horse takes, it is either done well or badly; and the rider can work positively, the whole time, to improve the horse. Exercise no longer becomes a dreary chore, because at any pace, the rider can be asking the horse to balance itself perfectly, to accept the bit, and to improve its suppleness and activity. The muscles of the horse will gradually begin to form in the right places, and the animal will become more beautiful, more tractable and, incidentally, much more valuable.

Appendix I

To make a simple arena—minimum requirements:

13 wooden pegs about two feet long

24 wooden boards, four to six feet long, four inches wide. (17 are for the arena, remainder spare or to mark the centre line)

Put pegs to mark corners and letters (two at A).

Drill ten boards at the end, remainder in the middle and fasten boards thus to pegs, with string or wire.

Fig. 52. Method of attaching boards to pegs

Put two boards at each corner, one at each letter, and one each side of the entrance at A. For dimensions see page 18.

The letters may be painted on plastic buckets, biscuit tins, wooden boxes or blocks—or if pegs are made large enough on the pegs themselves.

Mow the centre line (and the track, if the grass is rough).

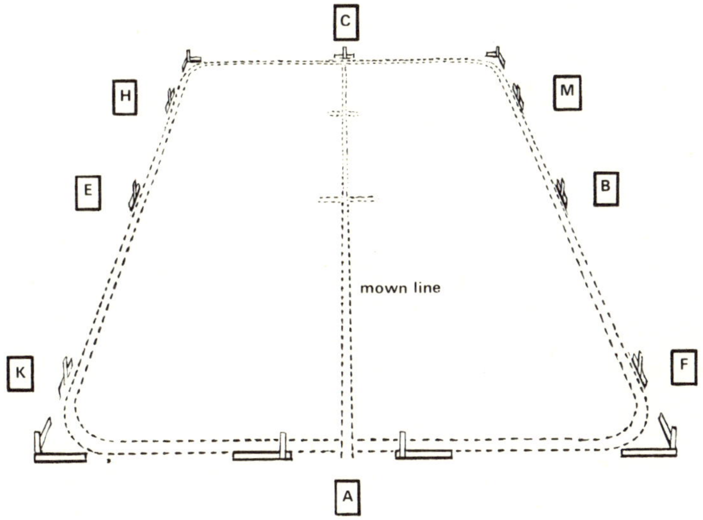

Fig. 53. A simple dressage arena

Appendix II

A list of useful books.

Manual of Horsemanship/Training the Young Pony/The Intructor's Handbook. (Essential facts clearly stated) *British Horse Society and Pony Club.*

Give Your Horse a Chance. *Lieut-Colonel A. L. d.Endrody.* (Full study, primarily for Combined Training. Author's meaning sometimes obscured by faulty command of English). (*J. A. Allen*)

The World of Dressage. *Neil ffrench Blake.* (International riders photographed in action, with useful comments). (*Pelham Books*)

Riding Technique in Pictures. *G. Harris and C. E. G. Hope.* (Helpful illustrations of right and wrong in many phases of riding). (*J. A. Allen*)

Development of Modern Riding. *V. Littauer.* (History of equitation, very interesting on the development of Dressage). (*J. A. Allen*)

The Trainers. *Ann Martin.* (Interesting insight into the methods of training by leading British and foreign instructors). (*Stanley Paul*)

Riding Logic. *W. Museler.* (Very clear study, admirable illustrations). (*Methuen and Co*)

Complete Guide to Horse and Rider. *Colonel Podhajsky.* (Full study by former head of Spanish riding school). (*Harrap*)

Olympic Dressage Test in Pictures. *Romaszkan.* (*Pelham Books*)

Encyclopaedia for Horsemen. *R. S. Summerhays.* (Useful compendium of riding terms with some illustrations). (*Frederick Warne*)

Dressage Riding. *R. L. Watjen.* (Full study, up to most advanced stages, and 'airs above the ground' translated by Victor Saloschin). (*J. A. Allen*)

Dressage. *H. Wynmalen.* (Full study up to advanced standard illustrated by photographs). (*Museum Press*)

Academic Equitation. *General Dĕcarpentry.* (Essential reading for any serious student of pure equitation; well translated, clear and logical.) (*J. A. Allen*)

Equitation. *Jean Froissard.* (Clear version of the French methods taught at Saumur.) (*Thomas Yuseloff Ltd.*)

Glossary of Terms

Aids Signals by which the rider conveys instructions to the horse.
  a Natural The hands through the reins, the rider's legs the seat and balance, the voice.
  b Artificial Whip, spurs, etc.

Accepting the bit The aim of the dressage rider, when the horse takes the bit willingly and softly, without resistance or opening the mouth.

Accepting the leg The horse responds to, and yields to the leg aid.

Accepting the weight The horse's back swings softly, and the rider does not bounce.

Balance The adjustment of the weight of rider and horse to the best advantage.

Back 'Hollow back', a condition in which the horse's head is too high, and the hocks are out behind (see fig. 36).
'rounded back', the opposite of hollow back, with the neck properly flexed, and the hocks engaged.
'swinging back'; a horse moving energetically and with a supple back, is said to have a swinging back, which is reflected in the action of the tail (see fig. 30).

Bandages Are not allowed in tests.

Bend The lateral bending of the horse's spine and neck when travelling in a curve.

Bits Only two types of bit are allowed in dressage—the snaffle and the double bridle, as follows:
Novice—snaffle

Elementary—snaffle or double bridle
Medium—snaffle or double bridle (as specified)
Advanced—double bridle
Variations of bit permitted are illustrated in Rules for Dressage.

Bit, above, behind, over the Faults, illustrated in figure 34, 37.

Breaking Term used when a horse breaks from one pace to another against the wishes of the rider.

Brushing boots Are not allowed in tests.

Cadence Rhythm with energy which gives the pace an extra quality, expressed by a springy and energetic lifting of the feet from the ground.

Canter See gait, and pace.
Canter, medium International term. A strong canter.
Canter, working International term. Equivalent to British "ordinary canter", but with slightly more collection.

Capriole A High School movement "above the ground" in which the horse jumps up and kicks out backwards—not performed in dressage competitions of any standard.

Cavalletti Variable bars over which horse is made to trot; invaluable in improving hock action.

Change of direction Achieved by a turn or incline on the move.

Change of rein To go round the school or arena in the opposite direction, or to change from one curve into another.

Change of leg To change the leading leg at the canter. 'Simple changes' are done by coming to the *walk* and striking off on the opposite leg.
'Flying changes' are performed by the horse changing legs in the air between strides at the canter.

Chewing the bit A good sign of relaxation and acceptance of the bit.

Collection A shortening and elevation of the pace by collecting the horse 'between hand and leg' bringing the hocks more underneath the body.

Contact The contact of the rider's hands, through the reins and bit, with the horse's mouth.

Counter-canter (Or counter-lead). To canter on the right rein with near-fore leading, or on the left rein with off-fore leading. The bend should be maintained over the leading leg.

Counter-change of hand A zig-zag movement, changing from a half-pass in one direction to one in the opposite direction.

Courbette A High School movement, in which the horse stands on its hind legs, with forelegs stretched fully upwards. Not part of any dressage test.

Croupade A High School movement, in which the horse jumps vertically, the forehand higher than the quarters. Not used in tests.

Diagonal (of horse) Diagonal pairs of legs, i.e. off fore and near hind (right diagonal) and near fore and off hind (left diagonal).

Diagonal (of school) Corner to corner (K to M or F to H).

Disobedience Wilful disobedience to the aids, e.g. wrong strike-off at canter, shying, bucking, etc.

Disunited Wrong sequence of footfalls at the canter; the front legs leading correctly, the hind legs on the wrong lead, or vice versa.

Extension A lengthening of the stride at the walk, trot or canter, to the limit of the horse's capacity, without change of rhythm (q.v.) or tempo (q.v.), or loss of regularity.

Falling-in Cutting the corners by dropping the shoulder inwards.

Flexion Yielding to the influence of the leg and the hand by flexing at the poll and relaxing the jaw.

Forehand The head, neck, shoulders, withers and forelegs.

Forging Clicking the hind shoes against the front; a fault indicative of fatigue, lack of muscle, or sloppy and unbalanced riding.

Footfall The correct sequence in which the feet come to the ground at different paces.

Freedom Free forward movement at all paces—the horse covering the ground with a long stride, willingly and without restriction of any sort.

Gait (see also Pace and Footfall). The horse normally has three gaits, walk, trot and canter; there are three more, the gallop, the 'rack' (a four-time pace resembling a very fast walk), and the 'amble' in which the horse trots with the off pair of legs and the near pair alternately (instead of the diagonals). Neither 'rack' nor 'amble' are acceptable in dressage. Incorrect gait, e.g. cantering in four-time instead of three, is a very serious fault. The gallop is not used in dressage, except as an exercise to free the horse's movement, when working in the open.

Half-pass Lateral movement in which the horse travels forwards and sideways 'on two tracks', bent in the direction towards which it is moving. The full pass, in which the horse moves sideways without going forward, is not used in dressage.

Half-pirouette A pirouette through 180° performed on the move at walk or canter, the horse maintaining the same rhythm and sequence of footfalls. (See Pirouette).

Half-halt The action by the rider of bringing the hocks under the horse in order to increase collection.

Halt Bringing the horse to a standstill, and remaining immobile.

Hindquarters The structure of the croup, thighs, and hind legs providing the driving force for the horse's movement.

Hocks, engaging the Bringing the hocks more under the horse in order to be able to increase the forward thrust and to lighten the forehand.

Hocks, 'out behind' The opposite of 'hocks engaged'.

Haute école or **High School** The classical art of riding, preserved in its highest form by the Spanish Riding School, Vienna. The culmination of High School riding goes beyond the most advanced stages of dressage to the 'airs above the ground' such as Levade, Courbette, Capriole and Croupade.

Impulsion Controlled energy (Chapter IV).

Impulsion, lack of Often indicated by loss of correct footfall in the horse's gait.

Jaw, crossing the A sign of resistance, when the lower jaw is protruded to one side or the other.

Lateral flexion Sideways flexion of the head at the poll.

Lateral movements General term for work on two tracks; including leg-yielding, shoulder-in, half-pass, travers, renvers, (q.v.).

Lateral suppleness See bend.

Leg, rider's, inside or outside The outside leg is that nearest the wall of the school or arena, or on the outside of any curve, e.g. on the left rein, the rider's left leg is the inside leg, the right leg the outside.

Leg-yielding A lateral movement in which the horse moves forwards and sideways, but is slightly bent *away* from the direction of movement (cp. half-pass, in which the horse is bent towards the direction of movement). The bend is only sufficient to allow the rider to see the horse's eyebrow.

Levade A High School 'air above the ground' in which the horse lowers the quarters, with the hocks brought completely under the body, and raises the forehand off the ground. (See fig. 27). Not used in any dressage test.

Martingales Are not allowed in tests, and should not be necessary for the dressage rider.

Medium walk, trot, canter International term, formerly translated by the F.E.I. as 'ordinary' walk, trot, and canter. But note that medium canter or trot is *much* stronger than the British 'ordinary' canter or trot. Not required at Novice Standard.

Mouth Besides the actual mouth, the word is used to describe the horse's acceptance of the bit. A stiff resistant horse, with open mouth, pulling, is said to have 'no mouth'.

Neck, broken (see fig. 39), **Neck, ewe** (see fig. 36), **Neck, upside down** (see fig. 1) Faults in head carriage, caused by insufficient or incorrect training.

Noseband Plain cavesson, or dropped nosebands, are permitted with a snaffle. A dropped noseband is not allowed with a double bridle. Crossed nosebands and other devices are forbidden, though the Grakle noseband has recently been accepted by the F.E.I.

Outline See Profile.

Overbending When the line of the horse's face comes beyond the vertical (see fig. 25).

Pace (See also Gait). The 'basic paces' in dressage are walk, trot, and canter. In Britain we formerly used the further sub-division of ordinary, collected, and extended paces. On the Continent, however, they use four subdivisions, as follows: collected, working, medium and extended paces, and this system has been adopted in Britain since 1975.

Medium pace is much stronger than our old 'ordinary pace', working pace about the same speed as our 'ordinary' pace, but with somewhat more cadence and activity.

A horse is said to have good or bad natural paces, which can be improved (or impaired) by the rider.

Passage An advanced movement consisting of an extremely elevated trot, with prolonged suspension. (See fig. 28.)

Piaffe An elevated trot, in which the horse remains on the spot. (vide Passage). (See fig. 28).

Pirouette A full turn of 360°, the movement being in fact a small circle on two tracks, the hind legs remaining almost on the spot, but maintaining the sequence of footfalls. Pirouettes and half-pirouettes are normally only performed at the collected walk or canter, or occasionally at piaffer.

Position of rider The seat and attitude adopted by the rider.

Position right or left The attitude into which the horse is put, with spine bent to right or left, in order to go round a corner. The horse can be ridden forward in position right or left as a suppling exercise.

Profile The outline of the horse seen from the side.

Punishment Can be by whip, spur, or voice, to show the rider's disapproval of a disobedience. Must be applied in such a way that the horse can associate it with the disobedience.

Quarters, in, out Hindquarters not following the front in the same track.

Quarters, lowering By flexing the hocks, the quarters are lowered, e.g. in rein-back.

Reward The expression of a rider's approval for a movement well performed. Can be by voice, patting, release from restriction, or by award of food.

Rein, inside and outside As for leg, inside and outside.

Renvers A lateral movement, half-pass with tail to the wall, the hind legs on the track, and the front legs inside the track. The horse is bent *towards* the direction of movement.

Rhythm Regularity of footfall, at each pace, maintained whether at ordinary, collected, or extended pace.

Riding-in Preparatory work, before entering the arena for a test.

Running An incorrect trot (see fig. 38).

Running reins An extra rein threaded through the ring of the bit, returning to the saddle. An extremely powerful weapon, capable of doing much harm, and forbidden in dressage tests.

Ruade A High School movement, performed by the French School —the horse kicks the hind legs high in the air, the front legs remaining on the ground (French also call this movement the croupade q.v.). Not part of any dressage test.

Serpentines Figures involving changes of rein.

Shoulder-in A lateral movement, in which the hind legs remain in the track, and the shoulder is brought in off the track, the horse moving forwards "on two tracks", bent *away* from the direction of movement.

Spurs Optional in Novice and Elementary tests, compulsory in Medium and above.

Speed The actual speed of the horse, measured in miles per hour or feet per second. (see Rhythm and Tempo).

Strike-off The act of breaking into the canter in response to the aid.

Suspension A period in which none of the horse's feet are on the ground. Occurs at trot, canter, or gallop (see Cadence).

Tail, swinging A sign of good movement (see fig. 31).

Tail, swishing A sign of resistance.

Teeth, grinding A sign of resistance.

Teeth, faulty May lead to tilted head, or uneasiness in the mouth.

Tempo Rapidity or frequency of footfall, measured in time (see Rhythm).

Tracking up Or overtracking—describes how, at the walk, the hind foot should come down on, or in front of, the print of the forefoot on the same side.

Transition The change from one pace to another.

Travers A lateral movement, half pass, head to the wall, tail in from the track, horse bent *towards* the direction of movement.

Trot, medium International term, formerly translated as 'ordinary' trot but much stronger than British 'ordinary trot'. The horse shows some extension.

Trot, rising When the rider rises at each alternate stride. Called 'posting' by the Americans. May be used for working, medium or extended trot, as specified in Test.

Trot, sitting Always used for collected trot, may be used for working, medium or extended trot, as specified in Test.

Trot, working International term for pace between medium (q.v.) and collected trot, in which a horse, not yet ready for collected movements, shows itself properly balanced, and with a supple poll, remaining on the bit, goes forward with even, elastic steps, and good hock action.
The equivalent of the old British 'ordinary trot', but with more cadence and activity.

Turn, right or left A turn of 90° on the move, executed as a small quarter-circle, without loss of rhythm or balance.

Turn, on the forehand To 'turn right on the forehand' the rider draws back the *right* leg and applies it in order to cause the horse to move his quarters away to the left, pivoting on the off fore leg, which should remain on the same spot. The horse is bent slightly to the right.
Seldom used in tests, but a valuable exercise for teaching the horse to move the quarters away from the leg. May be performed at the walk or from the halt.

Turn on the haunches A movement at the halt, in which the horse, bent in the direction of turn, pivots on the inside hind leg. Since the hind leg is static, this movement is seldom used, the quarter- or half-pirouette, on the move, being a more valuable exercise.

Unevenness Irregularity of rhythm or pace.

Unlevel The horse dropping more heavily on a particular leg. Often used as a kind word for lameness, which term judges prefer to avoid. A serious fault; if it is very pronounced, the judges may order the horse to be inspected by a veterinary surgeon before continuing in a combined event.

Voice A valuable aid, but not allowed during a test.

Volte A very small circle, 6 metres diameter.

Walk The various walks are as follows:—
ordinary, collected, extended, free walk on a long rein, and free walk on a loose rein. In international terms; 'ordinary walk' is called 'medium walk'.

Wandering Deviation from a straight line.

Wide behind A fault in action, illustrated in fig. 47.